YOU Are The CEO of Your Career:

Mastering the Job Search
In 10 Easy Steps

Mindy Stern

Note: This book provides information about how to advance your career with exercises that provide clarity and ideas that will help you to move forward in your career journey.

The author has used best efforts in preparing the information contained in this book. If you wish to apply the ideas contained in this book, you are taking full responsibility for your actions. The author and publisher shall in no event be held liable for any direct or indirect, incidental or other consequential damages arising from any use of this material which is provided as is and without warranties.

The publisher and author are not engaged in rendering legal, accounting, therapeutic or other similar services. If legal or other expert assistance is required, the services of an accredited professional should be sought.

Cover and Text Design: Stephanie Larkin

Published by Red Penguin Books, New York

ISBN: 978-1-949864-46-5 (print)

978-1-949864-51-9 (digital)

Additional copies of this book may be ordered online at
www.aimresourcegroup.com

For my awesome family with great love and appreciation.

Special thanks to my husband, Ziggie, whose unwavering support makes everything possible.

Table of Contents

FOREWORD

When Mindy Stern asked me if I would read the manuscript of her soon-to-be-published book, *"You Are the CEO of Your Career- Mastering The Job Search in 10 Easy Steps,"* I felt very honored. For several years, Mindy and I served together on the Board of the Long Island Chapter of the International Coach Federation, and I have always known Mindy to be an extremely knowledgeable, focused, and effective person, who has been a tremendous asset for our team's organizational success. I also know her to be a highly successful person, as a coach, as an HR professional, and as an entrepreneur.

When I read her book, I was delighted to discover that she is also a wonderful writer, with an amazing ability to communicate clearly and powerfully, with humor and insight, as she focuses her job-seeking reader on considering and mastering ten "Easy" steps which are really not necessarily so "Easy." Fortunately, she has the uncanny ability to make rather complex and sophisticated concepts clear and easy to grasp and, with the job seeker's commitment to following through, these concepts are well within the capability of the reader to master.

Mindy knows an incredible amount about the job search process, based on her years of experience helping organizations find the right people to hire and her years of experience helping job seekers learn what they have to do to optimize their chances of being hired for the jobs they really want. Her book is very well organized and systematic in presenting the ten areas that are essential to the successful job search process, but her presentation is never boring or dry; she provides lots of wonderful anecdotes and helpful hints, lots of exercises and examples, and lots of opportunities to practice what needs to be learned and mastered. I love the fact that Mindy speaks to the reader in first-person, throughout the book, making this more of a personal conversation with a warm and caring mentor or coach rather than what otherwise could have been simply a detached "how-to" manual.

If you, the reader, decide to use this book as a guide to work on alone while developing the skills needed to ensure a successful transition to finding the right job, you will definitely not feel "alone" through the process, because Mindy will be right there with you, every step of the way. And if you, the reader, decide to hire a career coach to help ensure personal accountability and ongoing motivation throughout the job-search process, Mindy's book will serve as the best possible foundation for both you, the job seeker, and your coach to look at and study together, for essential information, wisdom, and clarity in navigating what is inevitably a challenging journey (albeit one destined for success if Mindy's "10

Easy Steps" are integrated and embraced). I know that I learned a great deal from reading this book, and I will keep it close at hand when any of my coaching clients are faced with the need or desire to find their next job.

- Marc Miller, Ph.D., ACC

President, Long Island Charter Chapter, International Coach Federation

INTRODUCTION

The secret of getting ahead is getting started. - Mark Twain

Early in my career, my boss told me that I would never earn more than seven dollars an hour. He based this assumption on the fact that I had started my career after I had raised four children and had a bad habit of questioning the "why" of his decisions.

Years later, when I was earning many times what my former boss had predicted, I realized that the two characteristics that I feared would hold me back, helped to propel my career. First, my ability to organize, prioritize and problem solve started when my children were small. They relied on me to manage their many overlapping activities, keep them healthy and guide them in the right direction. Secondly, my passion to understand the "why" of every situation helped me not only to understand human nature, but also the rationale behind many of the circumstances I faced during my career. I have often used these qualities to help me on my career journey.

> As I progressed in my career, I have followed four guiding principles:
> - Treat every person with respect and appreciation for the strengths they possess.
> - Approach every obstacle as an opportunity to stretch and grow.
> - Reserve the right to improve every day.
> - Express gratitude daily.

I have personally experienced the anxiety of job loss, the frustration of searching for a new job, the fear of starting my own company and the joy that came when I realized that I am the CEO of my career. Once I realized that I am the only person who can control my destiny, many of the decisions I had to make became easy.

How to Use This Book

"You Are The CEO of Your Career" is a guide to help you take control of your career. In the book, you will find 10 easy steps to help you get to the next level of your career. In each step, you will find inspirational quotes, candid stories from my life and practical guidance to support you on your career journey.

I have included tips, tools, and exercises that I frequently use in my individual and group coaching practice. Since leaving my position as Director of Human Resources, I have coached many people to help them transition into great careers. You can use this book in conjunction with a career coach or you can do-it-yourself, using this book as your go-to resource whenever you are ready to transition to the next level of your career.

Whether you are looking for your first job or your last job, the easy-to-understand exercises will help you to assess your own knowledge and practice your new skills. While I have given you the space to complete the exercises within the book, you may want to start a career journal to document your journey and use it together with this book.

My goal is that this book will be your guide, to inspire and empower you to take control of your life and give you the confidence to be the CEO of your career!

STEP #1 KNOW YOUR PERSONAL BRAND

The journey of a thousand miles begins with one step. - Lao Tzu

I only visited a psychic once in my lifetime. As it turned out, she knew more about me in 5 minutes than I knew about myself in the previous 35 years. My husband had just survived a disabling accident and was unable to work. My son had recently been diagnosed with Juvenile Diabetes and my job as a Child Advocate in an elementary school was low-paying with no health insurance. I knew I had to make some changes to protect and provide for my young family. I visited the psychic reluctantly, but her prediction was prophetic. "I see you surrounded by papers at a large desk, with many people waiting to speak with you." I laughed about her prediction and quickly dismissed it. The day after the visit with the psychic, I applied for a job as an interviewer at a staffing agency and got the job! Within a few weeks, I found myself surrounded by papers, sitting at a large desk, with many people waiting to speak to me!

I didn't know it then, but that first job at the staffing agency was the beginning of my career helping people to connect with jobs that they were meant to have. I quickly learned what made one candidate stand out from the others and what it took for someone to transition smoothly from one career to another.

Marketing Yourself

Whether you are looking for your first job or transitioning into a new career, there are basic rules you need to follow in order to be successful. The first rule is to learn how to brand and market yourself. Approach the job search with the same imagination, discipline and sense of adventure you would approach any new job.

Most of us will be employed by multiple organizations in our work life and may not only change jobs but also change careers several times in our lives. That means marketing yourself, career development, career exploration, resume building, and networking will become a permanent part of your employment landscape in the years ahead.

What is personal branding and why is it important?

A "personal brand" is language borrowed from the marketing world that communicates who you are in the workplace and reflects your professional reputation. Instead of marketing a product, your full-time job is to market yourself. Once you can articulate your personal brand, it will be easier to talk to people about your future career aspirations. Knowing your personal brand will make introductions to strangers more interesting and effective. You will also use your brand as you prepare your professional summary for your resume. It is important to take some time to figure out a few ways to describe who you are and why people would want to get to know you.

Personal Branding Quiz

Take the personal branding quiz to get started – circle your answer below:

Do you have clear vision of your personal brand?	Yes	No
Do you know how to articulate your personal brand?	Yes	No
Do you have a well-defined area of expertise?	Yes	No
Do you know what is unique about your skills?	Yes	No
Do you know the audience you serve or would like to serve?	Yes	No

What is your Personal Brand?

Your personal brand represents who you are personally and professionally. It encompasses your strengths, your expertise, the impact you have on others as well as your character and behavior.

Communicating a strong and consistent personal brand is important whether you're looking for a new job, seeking a promotion, cultivating new business or advancing your career.

Tips to build and communicate a strong personal brand:

1. Google Yourself

People who search for you will believe what they find on the internet before they believe what you wrote about yourself in your resume. Here are a few things every job seeker should do:

- **Evaluate Your Activity:** Be sure that you know what recruiters are seeing when they Google your name. Objectively evaluate your activity on social media platforms, such as Facebook, Instagram, and Twitter to assess the image you project. If you post about controversial topics, complain about your employer or include inappropriate photos, it can negatively affect your professional image and your ability to secure a new job.

- **Check Privacy Settings:** Although your account may be private, there are a variety of ways that people can see your content. Check your privacy settings on each social media platform. Remember that although these may be personal accounts, it's important that the impression you create does not contradict the personal brand you want to project.

- **Your Biography:** Many organizations post bios on their websites. Be aware of the places where your bio is posted, and make sure that it is an accurate, current reflection of who you are professionally, emphasizing your expertise and major contributions. Fix errors or misrepresentations as soon as you see them.

2. Understand the Power of Keywords

Keywords are traditionally discussed in relation to resumes (see more about keywords in Step #5). However, the power of keywords goes far beyond your resume. Keywords provide information about your skills, qualifications, experience, and accomplishments. Since your first interaction with your future employer will probably be through an applicant tracking system (ATS), your keywords are often the reason your resume either will or will not be read by the recruiter. However, there are many other places to insert keywords to make an impact during your job search. Here are a few:

- **Networking:** Often the people you meet while networking will provide the pathway to your next job. That is why it is so critical to understand which keywords can best describe your experience and skills and include those words in your conversation. You only have about 30 seconds to make an impression on a new acquaintance. Practice using keywords that describe you before your next networking event. Words that express skills such as collaboration, communication, and innovation will make an impact on your audience.

- **LinkedIn Profiles**: LinkedIn is the number one resource for recruiters to find qualified candidates. They will often find candidates with keyword searches. Therefore, when you create your profile remember to include keywords in your profile summary, job descriptions, and education section.

It is important also to include volunteer activities, board positions, professional affiliations as well as honors and awards.

- **Resumes:** Use keywords in your career summary, list of achievements, job responsibilities and education sections. These keywords should include both hard skills such as programming proficiency or data entry speed and soft skills such as innovation and team leadership. Be prepared to expand on these skills during your interview.

- **Cover Letters**: Recruiters read cover letters to determine if you will be a good fit for their organization. They will look for proper grammar, writing skills and keywords that fit the job posting. I recommend keeping the cover letter short and using bullet points to highlight the skills that will interest the recruiter for the position you desire.

- **Interviews:** Once you design your resume with keywords it will be easy to include them in your interview as well. Listen carefully to the questions and respond in a thoughtful manner. A simple keyword or phrase can communicate your experience in a way that will differentiate yourself from the competition.

- **Thank You Emails**: When hiring managers are deciding between two equally qualified candidates, they may use your follow-up skills to make a hiring decision. So be sure to follow up within 24 hours of your interview with a well-crafted email to show your interest and be sure to include the keywords that were discussed in your interview.

If you know how to use keywords you will be able to showcase your experience and advance your career in a meaningful way.

List 5 keywords that describe your unique qualities, skills or experience:

_____

_____

_____

_____

_____

---

3. Use LinkedIn to Your Advantage

With over 500 million registered members, LinkedIn is your best opportunity to reach many thousands of professionals who may be looking for your unique skill set. I am always surprised at how many people resist using LinkedIn appropriately. If you are serious about your job search, then your LinkedIn profile must be a professional representation of who you are and what you do. Utilize LinkedIn to find new business prospects and opportunities for career growth. Here are a few things to focus on when you review your LinkedIn profile:

- **Your Profile**: Most recruiters use LinkedIn as their "go-to" site to find candidates for open jobs. Make sure you have a headline that describes what you do, a summary that ties together your major strengths and achievements and a current, professional-looking headshot. Your profile should also include your most recent jobs, board or volunteer positions, certifications and publications. Your profile should not be a duplicate of your resume. Rather, it should be a way to tell your story showing your key responsibilities, achievements and results.

- **Your Network**: Build your connections steadily. Make sure to personalize your requests to connect with others so that your contacts know that you are sincere about building a relationship. Remember to send invitations to people that you meet through networking, clubs, work and school. You never know who has connections that may be important to your career growth.

- **Recommendations:** Don't forget to request recommendations from your connections. Your recommendations will help future employers to understand who you are and why you would be an asset to their organization. You can also recommend others in your network who have been valuable resources to you.

- **Your Articles and Activity:** Showcase your expertise by writing an article or sharing a post that highlights your knowledge. The content you post will give you credibility and can position you as an authority in your field.

- **Your Groups:** Join groups to grow your network and increase your knowledge of areas that are important to you. Become an active participant in your groups to increase your credibility in your field.

4. Assess Your Appearance

Your appearance is an important reflection of your personal brand. Take the time to stand in front of the mirror and make an honest assessment of what you see. If you're not sure if your appearance is the best reflection of your personal brand, ask a friend or colleague for their honest opinion.

- **Your Smile:** Is your smile warm and engaging? Do you need to make an appointment with your dentist to make your smile shine?

- **Your Shoes:** Look at your shoes in the daylight. Scuffed, ripped or old-fashioned shoes tell people a lot about how you feel about yourself.

- **Your Clothing:** Assess your wardrobe to be sure that it is appropriate for the type of position you want to get. Applying for a position at a bank will require a different type of attire than a position at a start-up tech company. Note: regardless of how casual the environment is, your attire should always be clean, unwrinkled and odor-free.

5. Email and Voicemail

The way in which you communicate is a strong reflection of your personal brand. Make sure that you are demonstrating a polished, professional brand with the following tips:

- **Voice Mail:** Listen to your outgoing voice mail. Will you be proud if a recruiter calls when you are not available? Make your personal voicemail sound inviting and professional.

- **Email Address:** Does your personal email address look professional? Many job seekers create an email that is used specifically for the job search. Eliminate email addresses that sound juvenile or unprofessional. TweetyBird@hotmail.com may have been fine when you were in college, but it does not convey professionalism when you are applying for your next job.

- **Details Matter:** Pay attention to detail when sending emails. How you respond to an email will give the reader insight into who you are and what type of employee you will be. If you have typos, sloppy formatting, incorrect grammar or broken links in your email, it suggests a lack of care for your work.

- **Timeliness:** Timeliness when responding to emails is important. Waiting several days or weeks to reply to an email is a clear indication that you have not made that email a priority. Whenever possible, respond to emails within one day.

6. Positive Participation

Your personal brand is represented by your actions. Follow these tips to show others you are an active participant in your career growth:

- **Active Participation:** Actively participating and contributing to the conversation in meetings, networking events or social media groups demonstrates that you are engaged and care about your work.

- **Be Interested and Interesting:** If you appear distracted or disinterested while others are speaking, or spend too much time talking about yourself, you may be creating more of a negative impression than a positive impression.

You can control how people perceive your personal brand. Evaluating and improving the image you project is the first step you can take to advance your career. Go to the Action Plan on the last page of Step 1 to note the personal branding changes you want to focus on.

What is a Personal Branding Statement?

Your personal branding statement is a short declaration that tells others what value you provide, the audience you serve and how you do it exceptionally. Your personal branding statement is unique to you. It should become so familiar to you that it will be as easy to remember as your name. There are three things you should consider before you create your personal branding statement:

1. What makes you unique?

These could be qualities, skills or characteristics that describe why you are an interesting person or why you are better qualified than your competition.

2. Why do you do what you do?

In other words, what are you passionate about? Why should the listener care about what you do? If you are not passionate about your profession, then perhaps you should think about making a change so that you can speak enthusiastically about what you love to do.

One of my coaching clients is an insurance broker who has a passion for creative writing. When we first met, she had never cultivated this more creative dimension of her personality and felt that her career was uninspired and flat. She has now created a blog that combines her insurance expertise with her creative side, which has made a huge impact on her clients. People are drawn to others who can express the joy in their lives.

3. Who is the audience you serve or would like to serve?

Does your work impact business owners, or are you more focused on consumers? Are you involved in not-for-profit organizations or is your work more likely to be valuable in the for-profit sector? Does your experience include technology, or social services, or education or financial services or other sectors?

What is an Elevator Speech?

Your personal branding statement is sometimes called your elevator speech. Picture yourself in an elevator with the person you have been hoping to get in touch with about a career opportunity. You only have about 30 seconds to get his attention between the lobby and his office floor. You need a concise way to describe who you are and what you do in a compelling manner. You want to be able to grab his attention and prompt him to ask you to stop by for a cup of coffee. An effective elevator speech will differentiate you from all the other candidates. Think about what you can say in a short period of time that will pique someone's interest.

You may use your personal branding statement when:

- You meet a recruiter or anyone for the first time

- You write your career summary on your resume

- You need to introduce yourself at a networking event

- You are asked to "tell me about yourself" at your interview

---

Personal Branding Statement Example

This is an example of an effective personal branding statement:

> *I am an Event Manager with 12 years of experience developing company-wide events and creating dynamic communications for employees and media to promote those events and our brand image.*

This statement is effective because it:

- Quickly informs the listener about the individual's experience in the field

- Describes the value and the audience served

- Gives examples of previous accomplishments that offer insight into how the event manager could help another employer succeed

When networking, this Event Manager might add a question at the end of her statement to begin the dialogue with the listener. A question like "How can I help your organization promote your brand image?" will help the listener think about how to begin building this relationship and offer some next steps. An offer for a meeting or a phone call to further discuss would be a perfect way to begin to build a relationship.

Personal Branding Statement Exercises

Answer the three questions below and then use the answers to build your Personal Branding Statement.

1. **What makes you unique?** Take your keywords from the prior exercise and think about the skills and experience you have that others may value. Take a moment to write down at least 3 qualities, skills or characteristics:

   _____

   _____

   _____

   _____

   _____

2. **Why do you do what you do?** What are you passionate about? Why should the listener care about what you do?

   _____

   _____

   _____

   _____

   _____

3. **Who is the audience you serve or would like to serve?** Do a self-assessment of your skills, experience and who you would like to serve.

   _____

   _____

   _____

   _____

   _____

Now take your answers to the 3 questions above and create your Personal Branding Statement. Remember to keep it short! *Editor's note: If you would like to get a professional critique of your Personal Branding Statement send it to* info@aimresourcegroup.com.

_____

_____

_____

_____

_____

_____

_____

_____

_____

_____

_____

_____

_____

_____

ACTION PLAN

Based on what you have learned in this step, what actions will you commit to take that will lead you to career success?

_____

_____

_____

_____

_____

_____

_____

_____

_____

_____

_____

_____

_____

_____

_____

_____

_____

_____

_____

_____

_____

_____

_____

_____

_____

_____

STEP #2 GROW YOUR SOCIAL MEDIA PRESENCE

My mission in life is not merely to survive, but to thrive; and to do so with some passion, some compassion, some humor, and some style.
- Maya Angelou

A young man recently called me to inquire about career coaching services. He had been looking for a job for quite a while and couldn't understand why he was not being successful. When I asked him about his social media presence, he told me that he stayed away from that sort of thing and didn't even have a Facebook page.

While we were on the phone, I did a quick Google search and the first thing that came up was an assault charge from four years ago. He was shocked and upset when I told him I had found assault charges associated with his name. He told me that those charges had been dismissed and he had no idea anyone would be aware of them. It is not surprising that recruiters were staying away from him. No matter how great your resume is, if your social media presence conveys a negative image, recruiters will quickly move on to the next candidate. So, I encourage all my clients to Google themselves to see what comes up. You can be sure recruiters and your future employers will do it.

Since I provide outplacement and career coaching services, I speak to lots of people who have recently been laid off. I am always surprised at the amount of pushback I get when I tell them they need to have a professional social media presence. The following are a few of the myths I hear and the reality that I will share with you:

Social Media Myths vs Reality

- **I like my privacy** – The most commonly held myth is that you can maintain your privacy if you don't participate in social media sites. The truth is that no matter how much you guard your privacy, there is content on the internet about you. The fact is that anyone can say anything about you on the internet and it is nearly impossible to remove it once it is posted. You cannot control that. However, you can control the content you put out there about yourself, which should help to counter any negative items.

- **I don't have enough time** – The truth is that if you just spend 10 minutes a day, you can make a big impact on your personal brand. Spend some time reaching out to people you would like to connect with or research companies you would like to target in your job search. It is easy to make an impact by simply starting a blog, joining a group or sharing relevant information with your connections. If you don't know where to start, start by reconnecting to people you haven't spoken to in a while.

- **I can't compete** – I often hear this from people who are dazzled by celebrities who seem to be constantly promoting their own personal brand through numerous social media sites. The reality is that careless posts and compromising pictures often destroy the efforts of positive self-marketing. Using social media with a conscious, consistent and cautious approach can improve anyone's personal brand.

- **Social media is not right for my industry** – The truth is that most people use some form of social media today. Even if the industry you are aligned with does not actively promote its social media presence, its employees are certainly using it to some degree.

How Social Media Can Help in Your Job Search or Stop it Cold

Your social media posts will have a big impact on prospective employers. Most employers use social networking sites to research job candidates and use their findings to make hiring decisions. Hiring managers and recruiters are typically looking for information that either supports the candidate's qualifications for the job or for red flags that would stop them from offering the candidate a position.

Here are some reasons that employers may decide **not to hire** a job candidate:

- Candidate posted inappropriate photographs, videos or information
- Candidate posted information about their drinking or using drugs or weapons
- Candidate posted discriminatory comments related to race, gender, religion
- Candidate was linked to criminal behavior
- Candidate lied about qualifications
- Candidate had poor communication skills
- Candidate bad-mouthed their previous company or fellow employees

Here are some reasons that employers may decide **to hire** a job candidate:

- Candidate's background information is aligned with their qualifications for the job
- Candidate's social media postings conveyed a professional image
- Candidate showed a wide range of interests
- Other people posted great recommendations about the job candidate
- Candidate showed great communications skills
- Candidate had many followers or connections

Tips to use social media to your advantage

Since recruiters are actively using social media to fill their positions, it is important that you actively use social media to your advantage.

1. **Google is your new Resume:** Your presence on social media can give you a significant advantage over the competition, but it can also hurt you.

   - Spend some time researching privacy settings. If you're unclear about what content is publicly viewable, log out of your accounts and search for your name online.

   - If you create great content, such as blog posts, articles, videos, or anything else that can be displayed online, make sure to link that content to your social media profiles.

2. **Leverage LinkedIn:** Since LinkedIn is the most commonly used site for recruiters, make sure that you keep your profile up to date. Here are some tips to follow if you want an awesome LinkedIn profile:

   - Actively ask managers, coworkers and acquaintances to endorse you or write a short recommendation.

   - Consistently join relevant groups and participate in the conversation.

   - Actively share knowledge through posts and articles.

   - If you know your interviewer's name, check out their LinkedIn page to find common interests and shared connections.

   - If you are transitioning into a new industry, make sure that your profile reflects the skills that you want to utilize in your next job.

   - A professional picture is necessary for any recruiter to take you seriously. Putting a face to your name will help the recruiter remember who you are. Make sure the picture is clear, up-to-date and shows you in professional attire at an appropriate setting.

3. **Connect:** Use Social Media to engage with the brands, companies and industries that you want to be a part of. Follow companies that have an impact on your industry. Share their content or post relevant content to their sites.

4. **Personal Marketing Plan:** Create a marketing plan time budget – how much time can you devote to marketing yourself each day/week/month? Make sure to note this time in your calendar to hit your goals. If you decide that you want to spend one hour each day, then block the specific hour and stick to your allocated time. Use the **Career Development Plan** in Step #10 to track your goals. Remember to include "improve my social media presence" to your job search goals.

5. **Research:** For each social media site (i.e., Facebook, Twitter, Instagram, etc.) to which you belong, ask yourself if would you be comfortable if your future employer were to see your profile? Photos? Groups? Comments? Are you tagged in any photos online? Would you want your future employer to see them?

Answer the following questions to assess your social media presence:

On a scale of 1-5 (1= the lowest/ 5= the highest), circle the number that illustrates how effective you feel you are at using social media to promote your personal brand.

1	2	3	4	5

On a scale of 1-5 (1= the lowest/ 5= the highest), circle the number that illustrates how proud you are of the image others will see when they Google your name.

1	2	3	4	5

Action Steps: Whatever social media platform you are using, there are a few action steps that you need to remember to become an effective user. What are you doing consistently to increase your social media presence?

Check the boxes of the statements below that are true:

- ☐ I Google myself frequently to be sure I know what the rest of the world can see about me.

- ☐ I make whatever corrections are necessary to ensure that my social media image aligns with my professional image.

- ☐ I actively share my knowledge and expertise through posts and articles.

- ☐ I am sure that my profile looks professional and is free of errors.

- ☐ I am proud of the personal photo I use on social media.

- ☐ I build my network of connections regularly.

- ☐ I actively request recommendations for myself.

- ☐ I generously give recommendations to others.

- ☐ I join groups and participate in conversations that are relevant to my industry.

- ☐ I never share my user ID or password.

- ☐ I have created a personal marketing plan.

- ☐ I devote a portion of my job search time to develop and maintain my social media presence.

What's Your Next Step? Take some time to plan your next steps. After reviewing the exercise above, decide which action steps you will focus on first to increase your social media presence. Then create your **Action Plan** on the next page. Use the **Career Development Plan** in Step #10 to track your goals.

Here are some sample goals to help you start improving your social media presence:

1. Google myself once a month
2. Review my LinkedIn profile and improve it
3. Increase my LinkedIn connections by 10% this month
4. Join at least one LinkedIn group this month
5. Take a new picture of myself and post it
6. Write an article and post it on LinkedIn

Action Plan

Based on what you have learned in this step, what actions will you commit to take that will lead you to career success?

_____

_____

_____

_____

_____

_____

_____

_____

_____

_____

_____

_____

_____

_____

_____

_____

_____

_____

STEP #3 NETWORK FOR SUCCESS

Our greatest weakness lies in giving up. The most certain way to succeed is always to try just one more time. - Thomas A. Edison

When I was laid off from my job after 20+ years, I was completely unprepared for the journey I was about to begin. As Director of Human Resources, I had focused all my attention on promoting my employees and my organization and no time on promoting myself. I never gave much thought to what would happen if I didn't have my job. At that time I only had about 100 connections on LinkedIn and knew that had to change if I was going to find another job. I made it my mission to begin reconnecting with people I had lost touch with over the years. Within the first six months after losing my job, I had reached my goal of 500+ LinkedIn connections and those continue to grow as I build my business. I am not an advocate of adding connections just for the sake of growing your numbers. Keep in mind that anyone you invite to join your network has access to your existing network. So use discretion when you ask people to join your network and eliminate those who abuse the privilege of connecting with you.

What is ABR?

It is never too early or too late to begin networking. Networking is not just for people who are looking for jobs, and it's not just for extroverts. The skills you need to network effectively are skills that will be used throughout your life because our interactions with others form the core of our relationships. It's also likely that, over time, you will deal with transitions in your job responsibilities and question your job security. It is in your best interest to prioritize building and maintaining strong professional and personal relationships. I call this ABR or *Always Build Relationships.* Strong relationships help people live longer, happier and more fulfilled lives. When you focus on building and prioritizing relationships, you will be able to connect to jobs and opportunities that you could not reach by yourself.

One of my first career coaching clients was a young man who had graduated with honors from a good college and had spent the last five years looking for a suitable job. When we started working together, I asked him what he had been doing to find work. He told me that he spent 80% of his time searching job boards every day and submitting resumes. However, he had not had any success in even landing an interview. We quickly agreed that something had to change, and he began to learn how to network effectively.

At first, he was very hesitant to reach out to people he knew. He felt that it had been a long time since he had spoken to them and they either wouldn't remember him or wouldn't want to take the time to help him out. I explained to him that many people are quite generous with their time and if he was professional and respectful with his requests, he would reap huge rewards. He slowly began reaching out to some of his college professors who were happy to connect him to others in his field. He was pleasantly surprised at the favorable comments he received from people who genuinely wanted to help. It also boosted his confidence to know that people remembered him and his excellent work ethic.

Within a few months, my client was able to meet with some of those connections and found a wonderful job. He has been working ever since. His connections at his first job gave him the ability to explore career paths that he never considered while he was spending his time searching the internet for jobs. The internet is a wonderful resource but should only be used as one piece of your job search strategy. He is now a strong advocate for ABR.

The Benefits of Networking

Build a relationship first and do business second. - Jim McCann

Networking intimidates many people. Like most things that are hard to do, networking gets easier with practice. Remember that you have qualities that other people will want to learn about. When one of my coaching clients told me that she was much too introverted to speak to strangers, I suggested that she try a local Meetup that focused on photography, which was one of her passions. She didn't quite understand how that would help her to find a job, but she accepted the challenge and went to her first meeting. Within a few months, she had met several great people who shared her passion for photography. She began meeting them for coffee and photoshoots once a month. Her shyness dissipated when she spoke about photography and one of her new "photo friends" connected her to an influential person in her targeted industry. She was able to leverage these new relationships to quickly connect to people she never would have known had she not shared her passion with others.

Networking Survey

Many of my career coaching clients tell me that they hate to network. **Circle the numbers of all the items below that prevent you from networking.**

1. I'm not sure how to find the right networking groups.
2. I prefer to be in the comfort of my home.
3. I'm concerned that no one will talk to me at a networking event.
4. I hate crowded rooms.
5. I'm not sure how to explain what I do.
6. I am an introvert.
7. I am embarrassed to say I am looking for a job.
8. I don't know what to say to start a conversation.
9. I am afraid of saying the wrong thing.
10. I am uncomfortable eating or drinking in front of strangers.
11. I don't like speaking to people I don't know well to ask for referrals to job openings.
12. I am uncomfortable asking for a meeting with someone I just met.
13. I don't have the money to network.
14. I hate pressure.
15. I prefer to search for jobs on my computer.

What else is holding you back from networking?

_____

_____

_____

_____

_____

_____

Find the Hidden Jobs

The fact is that over 80% of open jobs are never posted on the job boards. They are either filled internally or filled with referrals from internal candidates. Many companies offer large incentives to their employees for finding qualified candidates to fill open positions. Their rationale is simple — if this employee is successful in our organization, we trust that he or she will know people who can be equally qualified and successful. So it is extremely important to network with people who can connect you with these "hidden jobs". With every person you add to your connections, you increase the probability of finding a hidden job through their network.

If you are not networking to increase your relationships, you are simply not doing everything you can to find job opportunities that may be perfect for you.

Tips to help you get started on your networking journey:

■ **Create personal connections**

Your networking goal is to create relationships, not necessarily to get a job. Strong relationships can last a lifetime and can be useful for so many different reasons. In many cases, a long-term relationship can last longer than your next job. When you find the common ground between you and the person you are speaking with, it is much easier to make a strong connection.

■ **Business relationships**

Instead of focusing on the "business" of a business relationship, try focusing on the "relationship". Think of networking as a potential new romance rather than a job interview. Just like a new love interest, your potential networking contact will zone out if your conversation is all about you. If a person takes the time to listen to you, they'll probably want to share their thoughts as well. So actively listen to them and try for an even balance of talking *and* listening.

■ Prepare in advance

Now that you have prepared your personal branding statement, it will be much easier to start conversations. For many people, small talk is the hardest part of meeting new people. Brush up on some current events or be prepared to speak about a current movie or television show you have seen recently. Stay away from conversations that include potentially divisive topics such as politics or religion. Here are some easy conversation starters:

- What three words describe you best?
- What always makes you laugh?
- What is the best piece of advice you've ever received?
- What was the first thing you remember saving up money to buy on your own?

■ Who do you know?

It is easier to enter a room full of strangers with someone you know. Finding a friend to join you at a networking event will help to ease your nerves. Just be careful not to use that person as a crutch. The point of networking is to meet new people and broaden your network; not to sit next to someone you already know and exclude others.

■ Don't be greedy or needy

People sense desperation and try to avoid it. Rather than making the initial conversation all about you and what you need, make the conversation about the other person and you will be surprised at how much you can learn. To make a positive first impression at networking events, conferences and parties, consider how you introduce yourself to others. You will want to build in your personal branding statement, but that should just be used to get the conversation started. When meeting someone for the first time, look for common interests and ask powerful questions about that person's job, company, interests, or industry trends. Learn how to be an active listener by asking engaging questions, and then asking follow-up questions. Everyone wants people to think they are interesting, and by actively showing interest in another person, you will look interesting too.

■ Use Power Questions

Here are some sample power questions to help you cement your new relationships:

- **"How can I help you?"** This allows you to add value immediately with a suggestion, a referral, or an opportunity, and it will establish you as a giver rather than a taker.

- **"Who else do you think I should be talking to in this room?"** This is a great question to ask a more seasoned networker who may be able to connect you immediately to someone at the event. It also gets the other person thinking about connections he could make for you.

- **"Would you like to get together next week?"** If you feel that you have made a connection, establishing a date and time for a follow-up meeting shows your interest and lets you know if the other person is interested in spending more time with you.

■ Reconnecting

If you are uncomfortable connecting with new people, reconnect with people you knew a while ago. If you have archived emails or old contact lists, start a methodical search for people you have not spoken to in a while. Reach out through email or texts to begin to reconnect. Then make the effort to meet for coffee or lunch to reignite those relationships. Remember to add your reignited contact to your LinkedIn profile and ask if they would be willing to give you a recommendation.

■ **Build Great Habits**

It takes effort to build relationships. However, if you create a habit of reaching out to a few different people each day you will become more confident in your ability to connect. Look at each day as an opportunity to improve. If you reach out to five people each day you will have the potential of connecting with over 1,800 people in one year. Even if only a small percentage of people return your calls or emails, your personal outreach program will help you to connect to more people than you know today. The more people you reach out to, the more likely someone will think of you the next time there is a job opening in their organization. If you make note of special events like birthdays and company anniversaries, that will give you an additional reason to reach out and cement relationships.

■ **Be a Hero**

When you meet someone new, take the opportunity to think of who that person could benefit from knowing, and then introduce them. You will look like a superhero. Follow up with them later to learn whether that introduction was worthwhile, and to become known as the person who is well connected in your sphere of influence. This will also make it natural for others to think of people who you should know to form a mutual connection.

■ **Join Groups**

There are many special interest groups that you can join that will advance your career. Many of them begin on-line and can give you a forum to speak to like-minded people. Other groups meet in person on a weekly or monthly basis to discuss shared interests. Meetup or other online social networking services are intended for people to organize and/or join group meetings. This is a great way to meet and connect with people who share your interests in your local area. Make it a goal to either join an existing Meetup or form your own that is focused on your special interest!

■ Follow Up

Some of the most important work begins after the networking event. If you do not follow up with the people you just met within 48 hours, it is unlikely they will remember you. Don't wait for others to follow up with you. Make it a point to say to the person you just met, "let's set up a time to meet next week so that we can get to know each other better". Then follow up with specific details. Get the reputation of being the person who has the best follow-up skills and you will become Networker of the Year!

■ Stay Relevant

Whether you are currently employed or working to find your next position, it is extremely important to keep your skills relevant. Stay current with changes in your profession, read as much as you can about new technologies and make sure to participate in ongoing learning and training. Networking can help with this if you are connected to the right professional organizations. Devote time each day to keep your skills current.

■ ABR

Remember to ABR (Always Build Relationships). A simple lunch or cup of coffee can lead to an important connection which can build into a business relationship.

What's Your Next Step? Take some time to plan your next steps. After reading the Networking Tips decide which ones you will focus on first. Then create your **Action Plan** below. Use the **Career Development Plan** in Step #10 to track your goals.

Here are some sample goals to help you get started:

1. Identify three networking opportunities within next month.

2. Contact five people each day.

3. Reconnect with someone I haven't spoken to in over one year.

4. Join at least one group this month.

5. Write an article and post it on a social networking group.

Action Plan

Based on what you have learned in this step, what actions will you commit to take that will lead you to career success?

_____

_____

_____

_____

_____

_____

_____

_____

_____

_____

_____

_____

STEP #4 – GET READY FOR THE JOB SEARCH

Choose a job you love, and you will never have to work a day in your life.
- Confucius

Before you begin your job search it is important to know yourself. If you understand what motivates you and what skills and qualities you can bring to our new employer it will be easier for you to find the job that will make you feel fulfilled.

Answer these questions to get started:

1. What are your most important career goals?

    _____

    _____

    _____

2. What are the key competencies (abilities, knowledge, skills, experiences, and behaviors) required to achieve your career goals?

    _____

    _____

    _____

3. If you don't have all the competencies necessary to be successful in this career path, what will you need to do to achieve those competencies?

    _____

    _____

    _____

Job Fit

Not every job opportunity is going to be right for you. When considering a potential job opportunity, ask yourself the following questions:

- Does this job opportunity align with my short-term or long-term career plans?

- If this job doesn't align with my career plans, are there other reasons to pursue it (compensation, health benefits, commuting time etc.)?

- Will this job give me the experience I need for future career growth?

- What is the reputation of the organization offering the job opportunity?

- Does this job have the growth potential that I am looking for?

- Will this job allow me to balance my life and my work?

- Have I considered alternative options such as temping, consulting, self-employment, or franchise opportunities?

Staffing Companies

According to the American Staffing Association, the staffing and recruiting industry provides jobs for nearly 17 million temporary and contract employees each year. Here are some compelling statistics:

- 76% of staffing employees work full time.

- 9 out of 10 staffing employees said staffing work made them more employable.

- 35% of staffing employees were offered a permanent job by a client where they worked on an assignment, and 66% of those accepted the offers of permanent employment.

I started my career as an interviewer in the staffing industry and I am a strong advocate for the experience temporary jobs can give to job seekers. Many of my temporary associates told me that I had changed their lives, thanks to the experience they were able to get through the staffing agency. I have received flowers, gifts and thank you notes from many grateful associates who were offered full-time employment at one of our client sites.

The goal of the staffing agency is to match temporary associates with the needs of their clients for specific jobs. Many companies rely on staffing agencies to fill short term positions for full time employees who are on leave, or for long term assignments to complete large projects that may last for many months.

One of our largest clients was looking for hundreds of telemarketers to fill outbound sales positions. We did not have enough temporary associates in our database to fulfill their needs, so I created a Telemarketing 101 training class. The class focused on the telemarketing skills our client required to fill the open positions. I invited all our temporary associates who had good data entry skills to attend the class. Over a period of several weeks, I trained the associates on effective communication skills, practiced active listening techniques, and provided best customer service practices. The associates did so well in the Telemarketing 101 class that I invited the client to observe our final class. The client was so impressed that he hired a few associates that night. We repeated our Telemarketing 101 class until we were able to fill over 400 positions for our client, and became known as the agency of choice for anyone who wanted this type of role. As a result of our classes, many of our temporary associates received offers of full-time employment with the client.

This is the type of experience that can change lives and careers. I am grateful for my experience in the staffing industry and often recommend that my career coaching clients apply for positions with a reputable staffing agency. Taking the time to work in a variety of industries or in multiple positions will give you the experience you may need to transition to a new career or find the type of job you are looking for.

Are you ready for a career transition?

Many people realize that the skills they have mastered could be transferable to other, more rewarding career paths. If you are ready to transition to a different career, follow these simple guidelines:

- **Strengths** – Make a list of your strengths that includes skills you have acquired, talents you possess, the expertise you have developed and areas that you are passionate about. In addition, think about the areas you would like to develop.

- **Research** – Before you decide to change jobs do as much research as possible about various types of industries and career paths. Speak with your contacts to see what opportunities are available in their organizations. Research the job boards to see what positions interest you. Take a few courses relevant to the desired industry to add to your knowledge base.

- **Speak to trusted advisors** – Think about people who you trust to discuss the pros and cons of various career paths. If you don't have connections with people who have the expertise you need, find a qualified career coach to guide you on this journey.

- **Financial considerations** – Sometimes shifting careers might require a step down from your current salary level. Make sure that your finances can support a reduction and consider if the risks outweigh the potential rewards.

- **Resume development** – Read your resume as if you were a hiring manager in the new industry. How do your skills match the job descriptions of the positions you would like to have? Fine-tune your resume and cover letter to focus on your transferable skills to convince a hiring manager to consider your application.

- **Be Confident** – Practice answering the question: "Why do you think you are qualified for this position?" Focus on the fact that while you are new to the industry, you have solved the same type of problems, used similar technology and successfully managed people at the same level as the new position.

Understanding your strengths and considering how to develop and transfer your skills to another industry will put you in a good position to achieve your goal.

What Are Your Employment Qualifications?

Now that you have thought about what you are looking for in terms of your next job, take a moment to think about the benefits you brought to your prior organization. The answers to these questions will help you to create Accomplishment Statements you will need for your resume and interview.

Ask yourself the following questions and answer below:

1. What have I accomplished in previous positions that I am most proud of?

_____

_____

_____

_____

_____

2. How have I exceeded expectations in former roles?

_____

_____

_____

_____

_____

---

3. What changes have I implemented that saved either time, resources or money?

_____

_____

_____

_____

_____

_____

4. Was I ever recognized for my contribution to an organization?

_____

_____

_____

_____

_____

_____

5. Have I ever taken on a leadership role?

_____

_____

_____

_____

_____

_____

Exercises to Understand Yourself

Before you take the next step in your career it is important to know what you enjoy doing and what motivates you. This will help you to determine which job opportunities you want to pursue.

1. What Do You Enjoy Doing?

What have you done in your career that you do well and enjoy doing? Even if you don't like your job and want to leave, think about the specific functions that you have enjoyed. These are the things you should be looking for in your next job.

Examples may include writing, coaching others, analyzing data, leading teams, doing research, solving problems, organizing events, planning projects, etc.

These are the types of tasks I would like to do in my next job:

_____

_____

_____

_____

_____

_____

_____

_____

_____

_____

_____

_____

_____

2. What Motivates You?

People who feel motivated at work will feel more fulfilled and therefore will be happier. Learn what matters most to you by ranking each category from 1 (very high motivator) to 10 (very low motivator). Use each number once.

_____ Ability to lead/influence others

_____ Career development/growth opportunities

_____ Compensation/benefits

_____ Feeling appreciated/recognition/praise

_____ Job security

_____ Meaningful/interesting/purposeful work

_____ My manager/organizational leadership

_____ Opportunities to learn/increase knowledge

_____ Social interaction with co-workers

_____ Task accomplishment/problem solving

Tips to Remember:

- People who feel motivated at work will feel happier and be more productive.

- In order to be self-motivated, you need to be clear about what you want in life and in your career.

- When you understand what motivates you and what you are passionate about it will be easier to set and achieve your career goals.

As Steve Jobs said, _"Your work is going to fill a large part of your life, and the only way to be truly satisfied is to do what you believe is great work. And the only way to do great work is to love what you do. If you haven't found it yet, keep looking. Don't settle. As with all matters of the heart, you'll know when you find it."_

Job Search Quiz

There are many misconceptions about the job search. Let's see how much you know! Circle all the numbers that are TRUE.

1. It is a waste of time to Google myself.

2. My LinkedIn profile is not as important as my resume.

3. At least 65% of new positions are found through networking and personal contacts.

4. The first five minutes of the interview are the most important.

5. If the salary offered is not what you want, there is no point interviewing for the job.

6. Always use your former boss as a reference.

7. When asked to describe your background in an interview, spend no more than 3 minutes doing so, unless questioned further.

8. Your eye contact, posture, and appearance are important non-verbal cues that will influence the interviewer.

9. If you are a smoker, always ask about the smoke break policy during the interview.

10. It is important to ask good questions about the company.

See next page for answers to the Job Search Quiz.

Job Search Quiz Answers

1. It is a waste of time to Google myself.

   FALSE. Google IS your new resume, so it is important that it reflects your knowledge, skills, and abilities.

2. My LinkedIn profile is not as important as my resume.

   FALSE. Remember that most recruiters use LinkedIn for recruiting purposes.

3. At least 65% of new positions are found through networking and personal contacts.

   TRUE. Many jobs are filled before they are ever posted, so it is important to cultivate a large circle of trusted contacts.

4. The first five minutes of the interview are the most important.

   TRUE. Hiring decisions are often made within the first 4-8 minutes.

5. If the salary offered is not what you want, there is no point interviewing for the job.

   FALSE. Consider all the variables such as opportunities for advancement, learning new skills, travel distance, etc.

6. Always use your former boss as a reference.

   FALSE. Especially if the reference might be negative. Think about former supervisors or colleagues who would give you great references.

7. When asked to describe your background in an interview, spend no more than 3 minutes doing so, unless questioned further.

   TRUE. Include your unique background and your most recent work experience. Do not include information about hobbies, family or personal interests.

8. Your eye contact, posture, and appearance are important non-verbal cues that will influence the interviewer.

   TRUE. Maintaining good eye contact as well as proper posture and appearance demonstrate confidence and interest in the position.

9. If you are a smoker, always ask about the smoke break policy during the interview.

   FALSE. Questions about vacation, breaks and time off can wait until you get a job offer. They don't belong at the interview.

10. It is important to ask good questions about the company.

    TRUE. Good questions show that you have taken the time to research and have an interest in the company.

Scoring:

8-10 correct – you are a superstar
4-7 correct – you are a rising star
1-3 correct – you have star potential

Action Plan

Based on what you have learned in this step, what actions will you commit to take that will lead you to career success?

_____

_____

_____

_____

_____

_____

_____

_____

_____

_____

_____

_____

_____

_____

_____

_____

_____

_____

_____

_____

STEP #5 DEVELOP A RESUME THAT GETS NOTICED

Success is not the key to happiness. Happiness is the key to success. If you love what you are doing, you will be successful. - Albert Schweitzer

When I first began working in the staffing agency, one of the tasks I enjoyed most was trying to match resumes to open jobs that needed to be filled. I eagerly looked at each resume with high hopes. However, I was often disappointed in the skills of the candidates and quality of their resumes. I have read thousands of resumes and many of them were either filled with typos or seemed disconnected to the job the candidate was applying for. I vividly recall the resume of an applicant for the Director of Procurement whose only experience was a cashier at a local restaurant. I remember several applicants who consistently misspelled the simplest words. Recruiters typically spend about 10 seconds reviewing a resume before deciding to discard or keep it. Make sure your resume is worth the recruiters' time investment, so they contact you for an interview.

An insider's view of why a recruiter may not look at your resume:

1. **It's too long.** Keep irrelevant information off the resume. Most resumes should be 1 – 2 pages at maximum.

2. **It has typos**. Misspelled words and poor grammar tell the recruiter that you don't care enough to edit and correct your resume. This also reflects poorly on what type of employee you will be.

3. **It's not relevant**. If your resume does not include keywords that are specific to the job posting, it will not get read.

4. **It has an objective**. This is an outdated and waste of valuable space. Instead, use a brief career summary that focuses on your experience and

accomplishments and demonstrates the value you can bring to a future employer.

5. **It lacks social media references**. In many fields, social media has become the go-to way for establishing a candidate's expertise. Recruiters and hiring managers generally look for applicants who are social media savvy.

Resume Real Estate

Your resume real estate is the small amount of space you have available to impress your future boss enough to ask for a meeting (your interview invitation). Don't squander that precious space with empty words that won't move you forward in the interview process.

When you are creating your resume, think about the perspective of your future boss. What would they want to know about you and how you could impact their organization? Don't copy your job description! Your resume needs to tell the story of why you would be an asset to their organization. Start by thinking about your accomplishments, not your responsibilities.

Accomplishment Statements

Every bullet point in your resume should include an action word that demonstrates that something got better because you were employed there. These are your Accomplishment Statements. You need to demonstrate that because of your role in your prior organization something either improved or progressed. Ideally, every bullet will also have a specific numerical accomplishment which can be demonstrated with a #, $ or %.

Examples of this type of Accomplishment Statement are:

- Expanded client base by 60% within 3 months.

- Exceeded sales goals generating over $750,000 in revenue in first year.

- Decreased average shipping times by 35% by implementing computerized tracking system.

Don't begin a bullet point with empty words such as "Managed or Responsible for..." Every line on your resume is an opportunity to showcase the benefit you brought to your organization in your prior role. Use your resume real estate wisely. Use the sample Action Words on the next page to create your Accomplishment Statements. Additional action words can be found in Step #10 Utilize Resources.

Create 3 Accomplishment Statements using Action Words:

1. _____

_____

_____

2. _____

_____

_____

3. _____

_____

_____

Here are 26 Awesome Action Words

(You can find more Action Words in Step #10):

1. Accelerated	14. Grew
2. Achieved	15. Implemented
3. Added	16. Improved
4. Awarded	17. Increased
5. Changed	18. Introduced
6. Contributed	19. Maximized
7. Decreased	20. Minimized
8. Delivered	21. Optimized
9. Eliminated	22. Produced
10. Exceeded	23. Reduced
11. Expanded	24. Saved
12. Gained	25. Sold
13. Generated	26. Streamlined

Will Your Resume Get You to The Interview?

The purpose of the resume is to get you an invitation to interview for your desired job. No matter what stage of your career you're at, developing your resume should always be a priority. Having a well-rounded and compelling resume is the key to achieving both your immediate and long-term career goals. Follow these steps to make sure your resume gets you to the interview:

1. Tell Your Story: Your resume should tell a story about your experience and skills. When you send your resume to a prospective employer it should reflect the value you can provide. In most cases, it is best to limit your resume to include the most recent 10 to 15 years of experience. Employers are interested in your most recent experience and how that fits with their open position's requirements.

2. Keep Your Resume Updated: I am often contacted by panicked job seekers who need a resume created today for a job that just became available. Don't wait for the last minute to update your information. Once you have a professional-looking resume, it's easy to add a few relevant keywords and submit for the job of your dreams.

3. Customize Your Resume: Each time you submit your resume you need to take the time to make sure that it includes the specific keywords that are found in the job posting. Don't assume that two jobs with similar job titles have the same keywords. They often do not. Customize your qualifications for each job posting so that the recruiter or hiring manager will easily be able to see how you could fill the open position.

4. Gaps: If there are gaps in your employment history be sure that you can account for the time-lapse. Include volunteer experiences, courses you have taken, blog posts you have authored, speaking engagements and community projects you have participated in to show areas of growth during the time you were not employed.

5.Triple Check: Double and triple check your resume for errors before you submit it. It is a best practice to have an unbiased person read the resume with an objective eye. Most recruiters will not bother reading resumes that are full of typos and grammatical errors.

Types of Resumes

The stage of your career will dictate the type of resume format you should use. Select the one that is best for you. The three most popular types of resumes are described below. Remember that a resume is a living, breathing document that can always be changed.

- **Chronological Resume** – Lists your work history in reverse chronological order, with your most recent job first. Employers like this type of resume because it is easy to see your career progression and who your employers were. If you have a solid work history use this format.

- **Functional Resume** – Focuses on your skills and experience rather than your work history. Use this format if you have gaps in your employment history.

- **Combination Resume** – Highlights your skills and accomplishments first, then lists your employment history in reverse chronological order. Use this format if you have unique transferrable skills or are changing careers or industries.

Key Elements of the Resume:

- **Name and Contact Information** – Use a slightly larger font for this section but use a minimum of space. Remember to include email and cell phone information so recruiters can easily contact you.

- **Career Summary** – Start your resume with a brief overview of your experience, skills, and accomplishments targeted to the job for which you are applying. This is where you tell your future employer why they should interview you.

- **Employment History** – List the companies you worked for, dates of employment, positions held and a bulleted list of responsibilities and accomplishment statements that will highlight the impact you had on the organization.

- **Skills** – List published articles or books, transferrable skills, technology skills, and various languages spoken.

- **Education/Certifications/Affiliations** – Unless you recently graduated from college, the education section should be towards the bottom of the resume. List colleges, degrees, special awards and honors, certifications and relevant professional organizations you are affiliated with.

Keywords

Most organizations use an applicant tracking system (ATS) to screen candidates for job openings. The ATS is programmed to find keywords in the resume database. The proper use of keywords will increase the chance of your resume matching the skills the organization is looking for. To find keywords review the specific job posting and look for the words that describe the position. Then use the words that best match your skills and qualifications in your resume.

List some keywords that are relevant to your experience and will get you noticed:

_____

_____

_____

_____

_____

Resume Design

I am often asked which resume design is best to catch the attention of the recruiters. Recruiters have a job to do and they need to do it quickly, which is why it is critical that they be able to assess your experience, education, and skills in just a few seconds. Having a great resume format is critical to organizing your information in a way that will help you get noticed. The best designs are well organized and easy to read. Follow the Resume Do's and Don'ts on the next page to develop a resume that gets noticed.

Resume Formatting Do's and Don'ts

- Do use basic, easy to read fonts like Calibri, Ariel or Garamond

- Do use keywords

- Do include white space to make it easy to read

- Do use Accomplishment Statements with hard data using %, $, #'s

- Do use past tense for previous positions

- Do be consistent in your font throughout the document

- Do use a Word document saved as a PDF file

- Do title your saved document with your full name

- Do double check for grammatical and spelling errors

- Don't overuse capitalization, bold, underline and italics

- Don't use pronouns (*I, we, etc.*)

- Don't use more than 2 pages (in most cases)

- Don't include personal information about your age, interests or family

- Don't include dates of graduation from college

- Don't state the obvious like: *references provided upon request*

ACTION PLAN

Based on what you have learned in this step, what actions will you commit to take that will lead you to career success?

_____

_____

_____

_____

_____

_____

_____

_____

_____

_____

_____

_____

_____

_____

_____

_____

_____

_____

_____

_____

_____

_____

_____

STEP #6 CREATE A COMPELLING COVER LETTER

The road to success is always under construction. - Lily Tomlin

Don't Forget the Cover Letter

I am frequently asked if applicants still need cover letters. In most cases, the answer is yes. Cover letters are one of the most underutilized tools that job seekers have. The cover letter is often the first impression an organization gets about the applicant. Use your cover letter to introduce yourself to your future employer and let them know why you would be the ideal candidate for the open position. Remember to use keywords from the job posting in the cover letter.

The main purpose of the cover letter is to get the organization to read your resume. Therefore, the letter should be clear, concise and appealing. It should include the qualifications that the company is looking for in the job description and a brief explanation about why you would be an excellent candidate.

Key Elements of the Cover Letter

- **The Hello Section**: This is where you should grab the recruiter's attention to encourage them to continue reading. You can use your Personal Branding statement in this section and add key words about the specific job opportunity. Address the letter to the hiring manager's name whenever possible, rather than saying Dear Recruiter or Attention Hiring Manager.

- **The Why Section**: This is where you tell the hiring manager the title of the job opportunity and why you would be a great candidate. If you learned about the job opportunity from someone who works at the organization or have a mutual acquaintance, it is important to mention that person's name here.

- **The Time to Shine Section**: This is where you tell the hiring manager a few of your most impressive accomplishments and qualifications that relate to the specific job opportunity. Be sure to use keywords that are listed in the job posting.

- **The Contact Me Section**: This is where you give your contact information including name, email address and phone number. Make sure that there are no typos and that this information is clear. If your cover letter extends to two pages be sure that your contact information is on every page.

This following is a sample POOR Cover Letter. It does not give the recruiter enough information to want to read the resume and does not clearly explain what value the candidate can bring the organization.

Dear Recruiter,

I am interested in the Coordinator position you are offering. Given my experience and excellent skills, I would be a great candidate for this job.

My resume is attached for your review. Please contact me if you are interested.

Regards,

Best Candidate

The following is a sample GREAT Cover Letter. It provides a clear explanation of why the candidate would be valuable to the organization.

Dear Mr. Smith,

I was excited to hear about the open HR Coordinator role from Maggie Jones, your HR Director. I would be thrilled to be considered for this role since I know that ABC company is one of the top manufacturing companies in the United States.

Having spent four years working in the HR Department of XYZ manufacturing company, I have the knowledge and skills it takes to be an asset to your team. During my time at XYZ, I was able to increase HR efficiencies by creating an online system to track all HR files. This saved the company time and resources.

I would love to speak with you about how I can be an asset to ABC company. Please let me know when you are available for a short meeting.

Sincerely,

Mary D. Taylor

marytaylor@gmail.com

555-444-3333

Use your cover letter to show your next employer the value you can bring to their organization and then be sure to follow up.

REMEMBER

- Whenever possible address the letter to a specific person, rather than "To whom it may concern" or "Dear Recruiter."
- Mention mutual contacts, or the person who referred you to the job at the top of the letter.
- Match the letter to the organization's needs and your skills.
- Demonstrate your expertise by including knowledge of the organization and your field.
- Use keywords found in the job description.
- Use clear, readable sentences and paragraphs.
- Use proper grammar and spelling.
- Use Action Words (see Sample Action Words in Step #10).
- Get to the point and keep it short.
- Ask an unbiased person to read your cover letter before you send it.

Cover Letter Exercise

Select a job posting you would like to apply to. Write a brief Cover Letter to the recruiter whose name is Ms. Brown, explaining why you would be a good candidate.

_____
_____
_____
_____
_____
_____
_____
_____
_____
_____
_____
_____
_____
_____
_____
_____
_____
_____
_____

ACTION PLAN

Based on what you have learned in this step, what actions will you commit to take that will lead you to career success?

_____

_____

_____

_____

_____

_____

_____

_____

_____

_____

_____

_____

_____

_____

_____

_____

_____

_____

_____

_____

_____

_____

_____

_____

_____

STEP # 7 TAKE CONTROL OF YOUR INTERVIEW

"When you look back at your body of work, no matter what your career path, ... if you can say, 'This place is in better shape than when I started,' then you did good". - John Cena

I estimate that I have conducted well over 1,000 interviews during my career. I vividly recall several embarrassing/funny/inappropriate interviews (depending on your point of view) that I will share with you so that you can avoid these mistakes.

Here are a few applicants who did not receive job offers:

- The applicant for a payroll position who told me that he was there to get my job and then proceeded to spill his bottle of water on my desk.

- The applicant for a director role who told me that the reason he left his last job was that his manager insisted all employees get to work by 9:00 am.

- The applicant who arrived 30 minutes late for an interview and then spent another 15 minutes in the bathroom "freshening up". She was rescheduled for the following day and again arrived late – blaming her alarm clock for malfunctioning.

- The applicant who brought a scrapbook of her puppy's pictures to show the interviewer.

An insider's look at recruiters' pet peeves:

- Candidates who look bored at the interview
- Candidates who dress inappropriately
- Candidates who badmouth their former employer

- Candidates who answer a phone call during the interview

- Candidates who have no clue about what the company does

- Candidates who give too much personal information or ask personal questions of the interviewer

- Candidates who chew gum

- Candidates who keep looking at their phone

- Candidates who arrive late

Preparing for the Interview

Interviews may be scheduled in a variety of formats. They may be a traditional in-person interview with one person or a team of people. They may be a phone interview which is often used as a screening tool before the company takes the time to schedule an in-person interview. Or a company may ask you to record a one-way video interview that they can review at their convenience.

Regardless of the format of the interview, the purpose of the interview is to determine if your personality, communication style, skills, and experience will be a good fit for the job and the organization.

You only have a few minutes to make a great impression on the person who interviews you. Here are a few things you can do to be prepared:

1. Research the organization so you are familiar with their product and/or services.
2. Understand the job posting and be prepared to describe how your skills will fit the job requirements.
3. Develop accomplishment statements that demonstrate your experience and skills.

4. Prepare a few short stories that will demonstrate the qualities you would bring to the organization if you were hired (i.e., how you went above and beyond; how you solved a tough problem; how you helped a customer, etc.)

5. Think about any skills you may be missing from the job description and how you would respond with related transferable experience or future learning.

Your Accomplishment Statements

You learned that accomplishment statements are extremely important for your resume in Step #5. They are equally important as you prepare for your interview. You will be able to communicate how your accomplishments can be valuable assets to your new employer if you prepare great accomplishment statements.

Hiring managers expect you to have experience in about 75%-80% of the job requirements. They know that they will have to develop new hires in many areas including proprietary technology, brand recognition and various forms of specific software. When you are preparing for the interview it is important to think about not only how you will respond to questions about what you already know, but also how you will respond to questions about what you do not yet know.

Accomplishment Statement (Experienced): Select a job posting that you would like to interview for. Describe how you accomplished one specific job requirement in a former position.

Job Requirement: _____

Accomplishment Statement (Experienced): _____

_____

_____

_____

_____

_____

Accomplishment Statement Exercise (Non-Experienced): Select a job posting that you would like to interview for. Take one specific job requirement that you have little or no experience doing and describe how you would transition your existing skills to accomplish this job requirement.

Job Requirement: _____

Accomplishment Statement (Non-Experienced): _____

_____
_____
_____
_____
_____
_____
_____
_____
_____
_____
_____
_____
_____
_____
_____
_____
_____
_____
_____
_____
_____
_____
_____
_____
_____
_____
_____

Tips for a Successful In-Person Interview

- Research the organization to be informed about their products and/or services.
- Prepare a few questions in advance that show you have an understanding and appreciation of the job.
- Arrive at the interview about 10 minutes early.
- Dress appropriately.
- Shake hands with the interviewer and try to mirror their grip.
- Develop rapport quickly with the interviewer.
- Maintain eye contact.
- Remember to smile and speak with an energetic tone.
- Be a good listener and follow the cues of the interviewer.
- Sit up straight in the chair; don't slouch or rest on the back of the chair.
- Take time to process the question before you answer.
- Don't interrupt or talk over the interviewer.
- Be prepared to discuss your accomplishments in a concise manner.
- Have stories prepared that demonstrate why you would be a great asset.
- Show your willingness to learn about new technology or processes.
- Ask about next steps and the best way to follow up.
- Ask for a business card.
- Send a thank you email after the interview.

Avoid These Top 10 Interview Mistakes

1. Speak badly about past employers

2. Exhibit poor personal appearance

3. Appear bored/ annoyed/ aggressive/ tired/ disinterested

4. Show up late to the interview

5. Don't ask any relevant questions

6. Don't research the company

7. Chew gum or eat candy during the interview

8. Answer texts or calls during the interview

9. Have little or no eye contact with the interviewer

10. Falsify or exaggerate accomplishments

Remember to be honest about your accomplishments. When you falsify or embellish your accomplishments it makes it difficult to respond to interview questions and the interviewer will quickly know that you are not being honest about what you have achieved.

I once interviewed a director of sales who claimed to have increased sales by 25% in his former company. However, when I asked him questions like *"What was your target market?"* and *"What changes did you make to increase sales?"* he was unable to answer. It quickly became apparent that he was not being honest about his accomplishments and I ended the interview. Interviewers are typically skilled at figuring out who is bluffing or who is being honest.

The Informational Interview

If you are planning to change industries or are just starting your job search and have limited experience in your desired field, you may want to include an informational interview in your search strategy. An informational or exploratory interview is not a traditional job interview. It is meant to be more of a discussion and exploration of career possibilities. After you do some research about your desired field, you can begin to select people who will give you a deeper perspective about the field and share various points of view. You can find people who may be open to an informational interview by talking with people who have experience in your targeted field of interest, networking, LinkedIn or your college alumni lists. You might initiate an informational interview for any of the following reasons:

- You want to gather information about a possible career.

- You want to network and meet decision-makers in a specific industry or profession.

- You want to meet someone who could help in your job search.

Examples of questions to ask in an Informational Interview:

1. How did you get your start in your industry?

2. What experience do you think is most important to succeed in this industry?

3. What advice would you give to a newcomer to your organization?

4. Besides your organization, what other companies are leaders in your field?

5. Can you suggest anyone else I should talk to if I want to pursue a career in this field?

Typical Interview Questions

It's not practical to list all the possible interview questions you may be asked. Some interviewers consider themselves very creative and will ask questions like "If you were a piece of furniture, what would you be?" Other than answering honestly and professionally, it is difficult to prepare for this type of question. However, if you can answer the interviewer favorite questions below you are off to a good start.

- Tell me about yourself.

- What are your greatest strengths?

- What are your weaknesses?

- Why do you want this job?

- What attracted you to this company?

- Why should we hire you?

- What did you like least about your last job?

- When were you most satisfied with your job?

- What can you do for us that other candidates can't?

- What were the responsibilities of your last position?

- Why are you leaving your present job?

- What do you know about this industry?

- What do you know about our company?

- Why do you want to work at our company?

- Why did you leave your last company?

- How would you go about establishing your credibility quickly with the team?

- If selected for this position, can you describe your strategy for the first 90 days?

- How do you want to improve yourself in the next year?

- What type of additional training or exposure are you hoping to get?

- How would you describe your work style?

- What would be your ideal working environment?

- What techniques and tools do you use to keep yourself organized?

- What type of company culture are you looking for?

- What do you consider your greatest achievement at work and why?

Behavioral Interview Questions

Many interviewers will use behavioral interview questions to find out how you behaved in certain situations in the past. The assumption is that your past behavior will predict your future performance. Behavioral interview questions are specific and probing. The interviewer expects detailed, honest responses. If you are not sure about how to answer the question, ask for clarification. This will also give you time to think about your answer.

Examples of Behavioral Interview Questions:

- Give me an example of a time that you felt you went above and beyond the call of duty at work.

- Describe a time when your work was criticized. What type of work was it and how did you handle the criticism?

- Tell me about a time when someone in your department was not pulling their own weight. How did you handle it and what was the outcome?

- Tell me about a time when you had to give someone difficult feedback. How did you handle it and what was the outcome?

- What do you consider to be your greatest failure, and what did you learn from it?

- Tell me about a time that your supervisor asked you to do something that you disagreed with. What was the situation and how did you handle it?

- Give me an example of a time you did something wrong. How did you handle it?

- Tell me about a time when you had to deal with conflict on the job and what was the outcome?

- Describe a time when you were required to finish multiple tasks by the end of the day, and there was no conceivable way that you could finish them. How did you handle it?

- What's the most difficult decision you've made in the last two years and how did you come to that decision?

Make sure to prepare for this type of question and give yourself plenty of time to respond. Interviewers expect you to give some thought to your responses.

8 Things to Never Do on a Job Interview

If you want to impress your interviewer, never do the following:

1. **Show up too early or too late**

   You would be surprised to know how often job candidates show up late! Showing up late gives the impression that not only do you lack the discipline and professionalism to show up when you say you will, but it indicates how you will behave as an employee. Arrive about 10 minutes before your interview time.

2. **Dress inappropriately**

Unlike years ago, not every job interview requires a suit (although some companies do expect professional business attire). It is important to find out just how casual the work environment is before you select your attire. You should ask your contact at the company about interview attire as specifically as possible. Under no circumstances should your clothing be wrinkled, dirty or smelly.

3. **Use your cellphone**

Using your cellphone during the interview shows a lack of respect for the interviewer and the interview process. It also shows that you lack appropriate boundaries and the ability to focus.

4. **Lie or stretch the truth**

You should never lie on your interview - dishonesty is easily discovered. It is much better to be honest about difficult situations and then describe what you learned about yourself, rather than lying to cover up a weakness.

5. **Exhibit distracting body language**

This includes things like not making good eye contact, not smiling, fidgeting throughout the interview, biting your nails, crossing your arms, looking at your watch, playing with your hair, your clothing, etc.

6. **Show up unprepared**

Prepare for each interview as if it was your most important interview. Interview preparation includes learning about the company and the job description, anticipating potential interview questions and preparing thoughtful questions to ask the interviewer.

7. **Blame others**

   Try to keep the interview tone positive. Never place blame on other people for things that happened in your work history, especially former supervisors. Focus on what lessons you learned that helped you to grow professionally.

8. **Share confidential information**

   When you share confidential information about former companies you put your interviewers in an awkward position and show them that you lack integrity. Interviewers are trying to find out if you will be a good fit for their organization. They are not likely to be impressed by someone they cannot trust.

Checklist to Prepare for the Interview

☐ Research the organization

☐ Prepare your elevator speech

☐ Prepare your accomplishment statements

☐ Prepare a list of great questions to ask the interviewer

☐ Prepare appropriate attire to wear to the interview

☐ Get enough sleep the night before the interview

☐ Leave more than enough time to get to the interview on time

☐ Bring address/directions for the interview location

☐ Bring 2 forms of ID including 1 photo ID

☐ Bring your business cards if you have them

☐ Bring interviewers name and phone #

☐ Bring clean copies of your resume

☐ Bring pad and pen

☐ Bring all the information you may need to complete an application (previous employer's addresses, phone #'s, etc.)

☐ Bring a list of references with their contact information

☐ Bring examples of your work (if applicable)

☐ Remember to ask for the interviewer's business card

☐ Ask about next steps

Checklist for After the Interview

☐ Send individual thank you emails to each person you spoke to within 24 hours of the interview

☐ Address any important points that came up in the interview

☐ Customize each thank you email for the intended recipient

☐ Follow up within 2 weeks of the interview to check the status of your application

ACTION PLAN

Based on what you have learned in this step, what actions will you commit to take that will lead you to career success?

_____

_____

_____

_____

_____

_____

_____

_____

_____

_____

_____

_____

_____

_____

_____

_____

_____

_____

_____

_____

_____

_____

_____

STEP #8 GIVE GREAT ANSWERS TO TOUGH QUESTIONS

Effective communication is 20% what you know and 80% how you feel about what you know." - Jim Rohn

Turn a Negative into a Positive

There is no need to worry about the tough questions you will be asked by the interviewer if you prepare in advance. The secret is to always look for ways to turn a negative into a positive.

Here are a few tough questions that you should be prepared for since they are hiring manager favorites:

1. Tell me about yourself.

This question may seem simple, but if you are not prepared with a compelling answer, your response can end your chances of a job offer. Your reply can either signal the beginning of a great interview or cause a quick end to the conversation. Keep in mind that many interviewers decide within the first 4-8 minutes whether they will move forward with the candidate. Since this question generally comes at the beginning of the interview it is a perfect opportunity to demonstrate why you are the best candidate for the job. Don't squander the opportunity to impress your interviewer with inconsequential personal stories about how you like to travel or have great kids. An employer isn't going to hire you because you have children or interesting hobbies.

Focus on the specific job opportunity and think about what you would want to know if you were the interviewer. Tell the interviewer about your accomplishments and the experience that makes you an ideal candidate for the job you are seeking. Highlight what you are most proud of in your career and the value you can provide to your future employer's organization.

Proper preparation is key to answering this question quickly and confidently. If you don't know where to begin, refer to your Personal Branding Statement in Step #1 and remember to add specifics about how your qualifications will bring value to the targeted job. Now take a moment to "Tell me about yourself":

_____

_____

_____

_____

_____

_____

_____

_____

_____

_____

_____

_____

_____

_____

_____

_____

_____

2. What's your biggest weakness?

Although you may spend a great deal of time preparing yourself to discuss your strengths, many candidates don't think about how to discuss their failures. Hiring managers use this question to see how you react in difficult situations. What they really want to know is how well you will respond to everyday pressure.

Using canned answers like "I am a perfectionist" or "I work too hard" will likely turn the interviewer off and will not lead to a job offer. Before you ever walk into an interview, think about one or two of your weaknesses and then create a compelling story about how you overcame each weakness.

During our interview preparation session, one of my clients was struggling with how to articulate a weakness, which for her was a lifelong struggle with shyness. After some probing, she told me that she knew that her shyness was holding her back from participating in team meetings and from leadership roles in her organization. To overcome this fear she made the effort to volunteer to lead a team meeting at work. She was surprised to realize that she had a talent for inspiring her team members to set and achieve performance goals. She was soon asked to take on a leadership role. She was able to use this experience to explain her weakness and how she worked to overcome it. The interviewer got a clear picture of her perseverance and motivation to succeed and she was offered the job of her dreams.

Take one of your weaknesses and show how you overcame it to become better at what you do.

My weakness:

_____

_____

_____

_____

_____

_____

How I overcame my weakness:

_____

_____

_____

_____

_____

_____

_____

_____

_____

_____

_____

_____

_____

3. Why did you leave your former position?

Hiring managers use this question to see how honest you will be. What they really want to know is how professional you will be when asked a difficult question and if there are any red flags they should know before they consider making you an offer. The key to answering this question is to be as honest as possible without ever blaming another person. Here are a few tips:

- **Explain why you are not currently working.** If you were part of a reduction in force, explain that a group of employees was laid off due to the specific reason (i.e., merger, acquisition, budget cuts, etc.) Don't waste time on the details of the reason – the interview is about you, not your former company. If you were fired, explain the circumstances briefly, assume responsibility for the situation, and explain what lessons you learned. If you left voluntarily, be prepared to explain why (i.e., I was looking to join a non-profit like yours; I wanted more career growth; the commute was too long; etc.)

- **Never criticize a past or current employer.** Hiring managers will view you as either difficult to manage or will wonder how you will speak about their company if you are hired.

- **Don't use money as the main reason for a job change.** Employers look for candidates who are motivated by more than compensation. Focus on why this position will be a perfect opportunity to use your skills to help your future new employer. Include your desire for career growth and your professional development, but make sure your focus is on how you can help the organization, not how they can help you.

Explain why you left your prior job and what is motivating you to want a job in this organization.

I left my prior job because:

_____

_____

_____

_____

_____

_____

_____

_____

_____

I want to join your organization because:

_____

_____

_____

_____

_____

_____

_____

_____

_____

_____

_____

Tough Interview Question Exercise

The ability to answer tough interview questions takes preparation and planning. Each person comes to the interview with unique life experiences. Use the examples below as a guide to create responses that best reflect your own personal experience.

1. **Why are you leaving your current job?**

Poor response: "I cannot continue working for my manager. He is mean and spiteful."	Why: Never bad mouth your current manager or prior employers. It makes you look bad, not your boss. Plus, you don't know who your boss knows.	Example of a good response: "I would like to work in a larger company where I can use my experience to contribute quickly to the bottom line."

Your best response:

2. I don't see any experience working with the ABC system on your resume.

Poor response:	Why: The goal is to	Example of a good
"You're correct. I've never worked on the ABC system."	always turn a negative into a positive. Let the interviewer know that you are a quick study and that something you experienced in your past work history can be used to transfer knowledge into the desired area.	response: "While I haven't had experience working with the ABC system, I quickly learned the XYZ system in my previous company. As a matter of fact, I was able to train new hires on the system within one month of my hire. I have been working on this type of system for many years, so I feel confident that I could easily transfer my experience to your system."

Your best response:

3. What are your strengths?

Poor response: "My strength is that I am a hard worker."	Why: Don't waste a perfect opportunity to make an impression by using very general words. Focus on specific attributes that will leave a lasting impression on the interviewer.	Example of a good response: "My greatest strength is my ability to work independently as well as collaboratively. While I enjoy working with a team, I also have a strong motivation to succeed, so I like to start my day early to get a head start on any project I am working on."

Your best response:

_____

_____

_____

_____

_____

_____

_____

_____

_____

_____

_____

4. What are your weaknesses?

Poor response: "My weakness is that I am a night owl, so I have trouble getting up in the morning."	Why: No employer wants to hire someone who is going to have chronic lateness issues. Find something positive to tell the interviewer about yourself.	Example of a good response: "I usually have a great memory. However, sometimes when I am working on multiple tasks, I need to take a moment to prioritize. I find that taking a few minutes to plan my day will save time in the end."

Your best response:

_____

_____

_____

_____

_____

_____

_____

_____

_____

_____

5. What are your salary expectations?

Poor response: "I am currently making $56,500 and want to be earning at least $60,000 plus bonus."	Why: Whenever possible let the interviewer be the first person to bring up specifics about compensation.	Example of a good response: "I am sure we will come up with a mutually acceptable amount. I am flexible and would like to hear what your salary range is."

Your best response:

_____

_____

_____

_____

_____

_____

_____

_____

_____

_____

_____

_____

_____

6. Do you have any questions?

Poor response: "No, I think you have answered everything."	Why: Interviewers want to hear your questions. They want to know if you have done your research and have a good understanding of the position and the company.	Example of a good response: "Could you tell me the structure of the department I would be working in if I were to get the position?"

Your best response:

_____

_____

_____

_____

_____

_____

_____

_____

_____

_____

_____

_____

_____

_____

_____

ACTION PLAN

Based on what you have learned in this step, what actions will you commit to take that will lead you to career success?

_____

_____

_____

_____

_____

_____

_____

_____

_____

_____

_____

_____

_____

_____

_____

_____

_____

_____

_____

_____

_____

_____

_____

_____

STEP # 9 ASK QUESTIONS THAT WILL GET YOU HIRED

The price of success is hard work, dedication to the job at hand, and the determination that whether we win or lose, we have applied the best of ourselves to the task at hand. - Vince Lombardi

The questions you ask during your interview can make the difference between getting hired and not getting the job. Don't squander this opportunity by asking questions that will not move you forward in the interview process. Save benefit and vacation questions for later in the process. Use some of the suggestions below to show the interviewer why you are different than your competition and how you could be an asset to their organization.

Sample Questions to Ask in an Interview

"How does this role impact your company's mission?"
It is important for you to understand the reason the position exists before you decide to join an organization. There are several follow up questions to the interviewer's response. Is it a new role, and if so, why is it necessary? Is it a replacement role and if so, why is it vacant? The answers to these questions will help you to understand if this role will fulfill your career goals and if those goals align with the company's culture and mission.

"How would you describe the work environment here?"
The answer to this question will help you to understand if the work is typically collaborative and team-based or more independent. You may also learn about the company culture and what to expect if you were offered the position.

"What do you expect someone in this position to accomplish in the first 60-90 days?"

This thoughtful question shows the interviewer you are ready to start contributing to the organization from day one. Take notes during this section of the interview so that you can refer to them when you get the job.

"What do your most successful employees do differently than other employees?"

This question is similar to "How do you define success in your company?" The answer to this question can help you understand what specific behaviors will lead to your success and if you will fit into the new organization's culture.

"What do you see as the most challenging aspect of this job?"

This question helps you to understand the perspective of the hiring manager and will give you some insight into the types of issues you will be dealing with.

"What is the biggest challenge facing the department today?"

The answer to this question will allow you to think on your feet and possibly offer some solutions to the interviewer. Even if you don't feel you can offer a solution, you will learn what the organization considers valuable.

"Is there anything about my background that concerns you?"

Addressing objections while you are still in the interview will help you to secure the job. You can respond to concerns by explaining specifically how you would easily transition into the new role. In addition, this will allow you to address the objections in a follow-up note.

"What are the opportunities for growth and advancement?"

The answer to this question will help you understand the structure of the organization and how you could advance your career. This is a great way to learn about various ways to progress or move into different roles. In addition, the interviewer may offer information about how the organization helps employees with continuing education, training or professional development.

"What are the next steps in the interview process?"

If the interviewer hasn't already shared this information, it's important to ask about their timeline so you're aware of when you could be notified of a second interview or a potential offer. If they say that they have just begun the interview process for this role, you know that you will have to wait longer than if they say we will decide within the next week. This will also help you to frame your follow up strategy.

I suggest that my clients have five questions prepared and ask two to three of them, depending on how the interview is going. Being prepared with thoughtful, well-researched questions shows the interviewer that you are serious about doing well in their organization and would be a great new hire.

Sample Questions <u>NOT</u> to Ask in an Interview

You will have plenty of time to inquire about salary and benefits after you receive the job offer. If the interview team is torn between two qualified candidates and you're the only one who inquired about pay, they might get the impression that the other candidate is more driven by passion and meaningful work while you're simply seeking a paycheck. Those questions are important, but the right time to ask them is when you receive the offer.

Here are some sample questions NOT to ask during your interview:

- "What does this company do?"

- "How much vacation time do I get?"

- "What is your policy if someone is late?"

- "Can I change my schedule if I get the job?"

- "Did I get the job?"

Questions I want to ask the interviewer:

_____

_____

_____

_____

_____

_____

_____

_____

_____

Action Plan

Based on what you have learned in this step, what actions will you commit to take that will lead you to career success?

_____

_____

_____

_____

_____

_____

_____

_____

_____

_____

_____

_____

_____

_____

_____

_____

_____

_____

_____

_____

_____

STEP #10 UTILIZE RESOURCES

I never dreamed of success. I worked for it. – Estee Lauder

The job search can be challenging and frustrating at times, so it is important to utilize as many resources as possible. Here are a few that may prove helpful during your search.

Frequently Asked Questions

I have included a few of the questions I get from my clients regarding the job search. It is often helpful for people who are experiencing the same concerns to hear questions and answers to help gain insight and confidence.

1.What are recruiters really looking for?

- A good fit for the company culture – Even if you have all the qualifications for the job, the interviewer or recruiter may decide that you are not a good "cultural fit" for the organization. The culture of an organization is difficult to determine before you know more about the company. Do your research to learn if the company is a good fit for your skillset and your personality.

- An effective communicator – Interviews come in many forms. They may be video conference calls, or automated voicemail interviews, or video recordings, as well as the more traditional face to face interviews. Regardless of the method, interviewers are looking for candidates who listen well and respond appropriately in a clear, honest and succinct manner.

■ A problem solver – Recruiters want to hire people who can identify problems and solve them quickly and effectively.

2. **Why should I submit my resume to an online job board when it is just going into an online black hole?**

It is true that applicant tracking systems (ATS) sort through many thousands of online resumes and eliminate most of them. However, that doesn't mean you shouldn't apply. Learning how to craft your resume and cover letter and figuring out which job postings are most relevant to your field can give you valuable knowledge and experience. You never know when you will get the response you are looking for. Apply to jobs that interest you and have descriptions that fit your skills as part of your job search strategy.

3. **Should I respond to job postings from anonymous companies?**

Avoid responding to companies that post anonymously because of what you do not know. Does the job really exist? What type of company is it? Will this company help me to move forward with my career goals? It is important for applicants to research companies before they apply. If the company is posting anonymously, you cannot find the information you need to make an informed decision.

4. **How long should my resume be?**

That answer depends on what type of resume you have and your number of years of experience. If you have lots of jobs or publications, your resume will be longer than if you just graduated from college. However, the standard rule of thumb is two pages maximum. Certain industries require one page.

5. **What soft skills are most important to hiring managers?**

    The soft skills that most hiring managers are looking for are also the guiding principles of great leaders. They include teamwork, collaboration, problem-solving and great communication skills. So make sure that when you are preparing for your next interview, you build in examples of times that you excelled in these areas. Prepare short stories that explain how you put your skills to use in former jobs and show examples of how you will behave under similar circumstances at your new employer.

6. **Should I negotiate my salary after I get a job offer?**

    Congratulations – you just got a job offer! Should you accept the position at the offered salary or try to get more? Over 50% of candidates accept offers of employment without ever negotiating for higher salaries. However, most hiring managers assume that at a certain level there will be some negotiation regarding compensation, benefits and/or vacation time. So do your research to know what is standard for your industry and then respectfully ask for what you need to feel fulfilled in the job.

7. **Why didn't I get the job?**

    It is disheartening to get rejected from a job that you felt was a good fit for you. Don't focus on the rejections. Rather, look at each job posting as an opportunity to learn and then move on to the next prospect. Here are a few reasons that you may not get the job, even if you had a great interview:

    ■ **You are under-qualified** – While you don't need to have 100% of the job requirements listed on your resume, you should have between 75-80% of the skills requested. Be prepared to show how the experience you have can transfer to the open position.

- **You are over-qualified** – When hiring managers think you are over-qualified they assume that you will quickly leave when a more appropriate position becomes available. Therefore, they may pass over your 20 years of experience for someone more junior, with lower salary expectations. Show your interviewer that your experience will have an immediate positive impact on the organization and that you have a desire to learn and grow.

- **You don't have a job** – Some companies feel that employed candidates are more likely to be successful in their work environment. It is always best to begin the job search while you are still employed whenever possible.

- **You were not honest** – Many candidates feel the need to exaggerate the truth to compete for a new job. This rarely works out, since once your future employer finds out the truth (and between social media and the internet, finding the truth is simple) you will not get the job.

- **Your social media presence matters** – Most recruiters will do an internet search about their candidates. They will not likely move forward with people who have a negative social media presence. If your social media posts are not professional or if there are criminal or provocative messages associated with your name, the job will probably be offered to someone else.

- **The job was filled internally** – Many open positions are posted both internally and externally. When an internal candidate is found, often they will get preference over an external candidate.

Job Search Resources

Here are a few sites that will support your career journey:

- **Bizjournals.com** Features local business news from 43 different cities across the United States to help with your research.

- **Careerbuilder.com** Source for job opportunities and advice. Access career resources, personalized salary tools and more.

- **CareerOneStop.org** Sponsored by the U.S. Department of Labor, this website offers a variety of free online tools, information, and resources for job seekers.

- **Dice.com** If you are looking for a job in technology, this is one of the largest and best-known technology job boards.

- **Glassdoor.com** Search millions of jobs and get the inside scoop on companies with employee reviews, personalized salary tools, and more.

- **Idealist.org** Provides information about the non-profit world and connects people who want to "do good" with opportunities for action and collaboration.

- **Indeed.com** Post your resume and search for jobs on this popular site which includes tools for job search, resume builders, company reviews and more.

- **Job.com** Offers weekly job alerts, job search advice, a resume builder and job postings.

- **Ladders.com** Candidates seeking jobs paying an annual salary of $100,000 or more can gain access to screened openings after they've paid a subscription fee.

- **LinkedIn.com** This site boasts over 500 million members worldwide and helps you to manage your professional identity with a personal profile. Use this site to build and engage with your professional network and access job opportunities.

- **Monster.com** Users can post a resume, get career advice, see company and salary information and search job postings.

- **Simplyhired.com** This job search engine collects job listings from all over the web, including company career pages, job boards, and niche job websites.

- **Small Business Administration (sba.gov)** The SBA provides free resources to people who want to start their own businesses. The SBA connects entrepreneurs with lenders and funding to help them plan, start and grow their business.

- **Usajobs.gov** Use this site to get information about federal agencies that are hiring. You can search and apply for federal jobs, learn about unique hiring paths for veterans, students and graduates, individuals with disabilities and more.

- **Vault.com** This site features rankings of businesses, best companies to work for and an industry research portal which contains industry-specific articles and profiles.

- **Ziprecruiter.com** Search for jobs in your area on this site.

What other websites will you explore?

_____

_____

_____

_____

_____

_____

Sample Action Words

Achieved	Adapted	Addressed	Administered
Advised	Analyzed	Arranged	Assembled
Assessed	Assisted	Attained	Audited
Budgeted	Calculated	Classified	Coached
Collected	Communicated	Compiled	Composed
Computed	Conducted	Consolidated	Constructed
Consulted	Coordinated	Counseled	Created
Critiqued	Defined	Designed	Detected
Determined	Devised	Diagnosed	Directed
Discovered	Displayed	Earned	Edited
Eliminated	Enforced	Established	Estimated
Evaluated	Examined	Expanded	Explained
Experimented	Financed	Formulated	Gathered
Generated	Grossed	Guided	Handled
Hypothesized	Identified	Illustrated	Implemented

Improved	Increased	Influenced	Initiated
Inspected	Installed	Instituted	Instructed
Interpreted	Interviewed	Invented	Investigated
Lectured	Managed	Marketed	Mediated
Modeled	Monitored	Motivated	Negotiated
Obtained	Operated	Ordered	Organized
Oversaw	Performed	Persuaded	Photographed
Planned	Prepared	Presented	Printed
Processed	Produced	Projected	Promoted
Proofread	Provided	Publicized	Purchased
Received	Recommended	Reconciled	Recorded
Recruited	Reduced	Referred	Refined
Rehabilitated	Repaired	Reported	Represented
Researched	Resolved	Responded	Restored
Retrieved	Reviewed	Scheduled	Selected
Solved	Sorted	Studied	Summarized

Supervised	Supplied	Surveyed	Tested
Trained	Transcribed	Translated	Traveled
Tutored	Upgraded	Utilized	Wrote

Which action words most clearly define your work experience?

_____

_____

_____

_____

_____

_____

_____

_____

_____

_____

_____

_____

Setting Goals and Achieving Them

The most successful people use goals to effectively set targets for themselves. Use the tips below to help you achieve your career goals:

- **Set long-term, mid-term and short-term goals**: Your long-term goals can be many years away. However, if you set very specific short-term goals, they will help you achieve larger long-term goals. Your mid-term goals will help you to look far enough into the future to begin adding skills and experience you may need for your career development. Setting and achieving goals takes a lot of consistent effort that allows for gradual, and steady growth.

- **Write goals down:** If you don't document your goals, you will likely forget them. Use a tool like the *Career Skill Building Worksheet* on the next page that will help you to remember your goals on a daily basis. Then create your *Career Development Plan* to track your goals. Celebrate and motivate yourself by checking off the goals you successfully achieve.

- **Have realistic goals:** If you set unrealistic goals you will not be able to attain them and may become demotivated. Make sure you know what outcome you hope to achieve and be realistic about the amount of time you can devote to your goals.

- **Is it important to you?** Make sure that the goals you select are relevant and important in your life. Ask yourself – "If I achieve my goal will the end result be worth the effort I need to put in?" If the answer is "No", then move on to the next.

- **Set deadlines:** Set priorities so that you can manage your time effectively and don't be afraid to say no to timewasters. If you find that you cannot attain your goals in the timeline you have set, adjust your goals to be more realistic.

Career Skill Building Worksheet

What career skills do you need to improve? What resources will help you? What actions will you take to build those skills? Remember to track your start and completion dates. Use the **Career Skill Building Worksheet** below to track your progress.

Career Skills	Improvements Needed	Resources Needed	Actions to Take	Start Date / Completion Date
Personal Branding				
Networking				
Resume Development				
Job Market Research				
Interview Prep				
Other				

Career Development Plan

Document your short-term, mid-term and long-term goals on the **Career Development Plan** below. What skills do you already have? What skills do you need to acquire to get you to the next step of your career? What resources will help you to get there? What action steps are important to include in your **Career Development Plan**?

Current Job: _____

Desired Job: _____

GOALS	Skills I have	Skills I need to acquire	Resources Needed	Action Steps
Short-Term Goals (2-6 months)				
Mid-Term Goals (6-12 months)				
Long-Term Goals (2-4 years)				

Action Plan

Based on what you have learned in this step, what actions will you commit to take that will lead you to career success?

_____

_____

_____

_____

_____

_____

_____

_____

_____

_____

_____

_____

_____

_____

_____

_____

_____

_____

About the Author

Mindy Stern, SPHR, SHRM-SCP, ACC is the founder and President of AIM Resource Group Inc. She has extensive experience as a leadership and career coach, educator and columnist. Mindy is often a featured speaker at leadership conferences and workshops. She writes a monthly newspaper column entitled *Employment Matters* to educate the public about workplace issues. She is also a trusted Human Resource advisor for organizations that understand the need to comply with ever-changing laws and regulations.

Mindy's career spans over 25 years, including roles of Director of Human Resources for a New York City based financial services company and Senior National Learning Manager for a global staffing company. Mindy serves as a member of the Board of Directors and Chair of Board Development of SNAP (Services Now for Adult Persons), a non-profit social service agency that provides education and support for senior citizens. She is the past Director of Public Relations of the International Coach Federation-Long Island chapter. She is certified as an Associate Certified Coach (ACC) from the International Coach Federation and has a bachelor's degree in Human Resource Management. She is certified as a Senior Professional in Human Resources (SPHR) from the HR Certification Institute and SHRM-SCP from the Society of Human Resource Management. She is active in several professional organizations including Society for Human Resource Management (SHRM), International Coaching Federation (ICF) and International Association of Women (IAW). She is a contributing author in "HERSpectives: Rules and Tools That Build Successful Women - How I Created Work Life Balance".

If you would like to learn how to accelerate your job search, visit www.aimresourcegroup.com or send questions to info@aimresourcegroup.com.

www.ingramcontent.com/pod-product-compliance
Lightning Source LLC
Chambersburg PA
CBHW081822200326
41597CB00023B/4349